Sizzling

BARBECUE
COOKBOOK

KÖNEMANN

SUBSTANTIAL SIZZLES

Pepper Steak and Steak Vin Rouge with Herb Butter

Food cooked over coals or glowing embers has an exciting flavour and beef, veal, lamb and pork provide the basis for many innovative barbecue meals. When choosing cuts of meat to barbecue look for good quality lean meats.

Meats to be barbecued generally need little preparation. Remove excess fat and make small nicks on the edges of steaks and chops to prevent meat curling. Marinate less expensive cuts of meat to tenderise and flavour them.

Meats for barbecuing need to be an even thickness to brown and cook evenly. Steaks are best cut to about 2 cm in thickness.

SUITABLE CUTS FOR BARBECUING

Beef: fillet, rump, rib eye, sirloin or T-bone, blade and spare ribs
Veal: leg steak, loin chops and cutlets
Pork: leg steak, loin chops, cutlets and spare ribs
Lamb: chump, leg and mid loin chops, cutlets, shoulder, leg and lamb cubes
To achieve a perfectly cooked piece of meat you need first to sear the meat over hot coals for about two minutes each side, turning the meat once only. This firms the surfaces of the meat, retaining natural juices. Meat is then moved to a cooler part of the barbecue to continue cooking. For rare meat cook only a further minute or two each side; for medium rare meat cook a further 2–3 minutes each side (meat should be slightly springy to touch); for well done meat cook a further 4–6 minutes each side (meat should be firm to touch). The very best barbecued meats are crisp and brown outside, pink and juicy inside.

Steaks Vin Rouge

Preparation time:
    30 minutes plus
    overnight standing
Cooking time:
    16 minutes
Serves 8

8 rump steaks

Marinade

1 cup dry red wine
¼ cup olive oil
¼ cup tomato paste
1 medium onion, finely chopped
3 cloves garlic, crushed
½ teaspoon cayenne pepper
½ teaspoon grated lemon rind
2 bay leaves

1 Trim excess fat from steaks and flatten them to an even thickness.
2 Combine all ingredients for the marinade thoroughly. Place steaks in a flat glass dish, pour over marinade and turn steaks to coat them evenly with marinade mixture. Cover dish and refrigerate overnight, turning steaks occasionally.
3 Drain and reserve marinade from steaks. Cook steaks over hot coals for 6–8 minutes each side, basting frequently with reserved marinade.

HINT
Use any excess fat from steaks to grease the barbecue grill or hotplate. Hold the fat with long-handled tongs and push it over the wire grill or back and forth across the flat hotplate. This prevents meat sticking to the barbecue while cooking.

3

Pepper Steaks

Preparation time:
  20 minutes plus
  overnight standing
Cooking time:
  16 minutes
Serves 6

6 rib eye steaks
2 tablespoons cracked
  black peppercorns
1 tablespoon cracked
  coriander seeds
1 teaspoon garam
  masala
¼ cup oil
1 clove garlic, crushed

1 Trim excess fat from
steaks. Combine the rest
of the ingredients.
2 Place steaks in a flat
glass dish, pour pepper
mixture over them and
turn to cover each steak
with the mixture. Cover
dish and refrigerate
overnight, turning steaks
occasionally.
3 Cook steaks over hot
coals for 6–8 minutes
each side for medium
rare. Serve Pepper Steaks
with garlic butter or rich
tomato sauce.

HINT
After marinating and
refrigeration allow
meat to come back to
room temperature
before barbecuing.
This ensures even
cooking of meat.

Barbecued Lamb Cutlets with Sauce

Preparation time:
  30 minutes
Cooking time:
  10 minutes
Serves 4

12 lamb cutlets,
  trimmed
Choose a sauce from the
  following for basting.

Hot Sherry Sauce
½ cup dry sherry
¼ cup soy sauce
¼ cup chilli sauce
2 tablespoons brown
  sugar
2 spring onions, sliced
2 cloves garlic, crushed

Provençale Sauce
½ cup tomato paste
⅓ cup red wine
⅓ cup water
1 teaspoon oregano
6 olives, chopped
1 small onion, chopped
2 tablespoons olive oil

Herb Butter
125 g butter or
  margarine
1 tablespoon chopped
  dill
1 tablespoon chopped
  parsley
2 tablespoons lemon
  juice
freshly ground black
  pepper

1 Arrange lamb cutlets
on a platter. Prepare
sauce of choice.
2 To prepare Hot
Sherry Sauce: mix all
ingredients together in a
bowl. Spoon a little over
each cutlet. Keep
remainder for basting.
3 To prepare
Provençale Sauce: mix
all ingredients together
in a small bowl. Spoon a
little over each cutlet.
Keep remainder for
basting.
4 To prepare Herb
Butter: melt butter or
margarine in a small
saucepan. Add
remaining ingredients.
Spoon a little over each
cutlet. Keep remainder
warm for basting.
5 Barbecue cutlets when
required for 3–5 minutes
each side. Baste
regularly during
cooking, with sauce of
your choice.

HINTS
☐ Short loin chops
may be used instead
of cutlets.
☐ These sauces are
ideal for fish parcels.
Place fish fillets each
in a piece of foil large
enough to form a
parcel. Spoon some
sauce over each fillet
(or add 1 tablespoon
butter and chopped
fresh herbs for Herb
Butter) and wrap as a
parcel. Cook for
about 10–15 minutes
on the barbecue.

Barbecued Lamb Cutlets with Hot Sherry Sauce,
Provençale Sauce and Herb Butter

Sweet and Sour Barbecue Steak

Preparation time:
   30 minutes plus
   overnight standing
Cooking time:
   10 minutes
Serves 4

750 g boneless lean steak
   (3 cm thick)

Marinade

½ cup tomato sauce
½ cup red wine vinegar
¼ cup packed brown
   sugar
¼ cup honey
1 tablespoon soy sauce
1 tablespoon
   Worcestershire sauce
1 tablespoon Dijon
   mustard
1 clove garlic, crushed
freshly ground black
   pepper

1 Trim any excess fat
from steak.
2 To prepare Marinade:
in bowl stir together
tomato sauce, red wine
vinegar, brown sugar,
honey, soy sauce,
Worcestershire sauce,
Dijon mustard, garlic
and pepper. Mix well.
3 Pour marinade over
steak in shallow dish.
Cover; refrigerate for
several hours or
overnight, turning steak
occasionally.
4 Drain steak, reserving
marinade. Cook over
hot coals, turning once

and basting with
marinade until cooked
as desired (6–8 minutes
each side for medium
rare).
5 Place barbecued steak
on cutting board; let
stand for 5 minutes. Cut
across meat fibres into
thin slices.

HINT
To test barbecued
meat for doneness,
press the meat with
the back of a fork.
Rare meat will be
soft, a medium steak
springy and well done
meat will be firm.

Sirloin Steaks with Horseradish Béarnaise

Preparation time:
   40 minutes
Cooking time:
   16 minutes
Serves 6

6 sirloin steaks
1 tablespoon oil
3 cloves garlic, crushed

Horseradish Béarnaise
¼ cup vinegar
2 spring onions
2 egg yolks
125 g butter, melted
1 tablespoon
   horseradish cream

1 Trim steaks of excess
fat. Brush combined oil
and garlic evenly over
steaks. Cook over hot
coals for 6–8 minutes
each side for medium
rare. Serve with
Horseradish Béarnaise.
2 To prepare
Horseradish Béarnaise:
place vinegar and
chopped onions in pan,
bring to boil, reduce
heat and simmer
uncovered until reduced
by half. Discard spring
onions; cool.
3 Process egg yolks and
vinegar in processor
until smooth, pour in
hot bubbling butter,
process until smooth,
add horseradish cream
and process 30 seconds.

HINT
When turning meat
on the barbecue
always use tongs,
never a fork, as a fork
punctures meat and
releases juices. This
causes fire flare-ups
and it also toughens
meat.

Sweet and Sour Barbecue Steak and Sirloin Steak with Horseradish Béarnaise

Tahina Skewered Lamb

Tahina Skewered Lamb

Preparation time:
   18 minutes
Cooking time:
   12 minutes
Serves 4

750 g lean lamb cubes
1 medium cucumber,
   halved lengthwise,
   seeded and sliced
3 tomatoes, chopped
½ cup chopped parsley
4 spring onions,
   chopped
½ cup tahina

200 g carton low-fat
   yoghurt
1 clove garlic, crushed
juice of 1 lemon
¼ cup chopped parsley,
   extra
pinch cayenne pepper
pinch paprika
¼ teaspoon ground
   cumin
crusty bread rolls

1   Thread lamb cubes
onto 8–12 oiled
skewers.
2   Toss cucumber,
tomatoes, parsley and
spring onions in a salad
bowl. Refrigerate.
3   Place kebabs on
barbecue, cook 10–12

minutes, turning
occasionally. Lightly
brush with oil if they
become too dry.
4   Meanwhile, combine
tahina, yoghurt, garlic,
lemon juice, extra
parsley and spices.
5   Serve kebabs with
tahina dressing,
cucumber salad and
crusty bread rolls.

HINT
Lamb skewers can be
brushed with a
mixture of oil, lemon
juice and dill while
cooking.

Oriental Veal Sticks

Preparation time:
  6 minutes
Cooking time:
  15 minutes
Serves 4

750 g veal strips
½ cup plum sauce
2 teaspoons soy sauce
1 clove garlic, crushed
½ teaspoon grated fresh
  ginger
¼ teaspoon minced
  chilli

1 Thread meat onto 8 bamboo skewers.
2 Combine plum and soy sauces, garlic, ginger and chilli. Brush kebabs with chilli-plum mixture. Barbecue kebabs over hot coals 3–4 minutes each side, brushing constantly with sauce.

3 Serve veal sticks with brown rice and salad. Any leftover baste may be used as a dipping sauce.

HINT
Bottled Chinese plum sauce is best used for this recipe. It is available from speciality Asian stores and some supermarkets.

Oriental Veal Sticks

Mexican-Style Beef Spare Ribs

Preparation time:
  1 hour
Cooking time:
  15 minutes
Serves 4

1.5 kg beef spare ribs
2 bay leaves
1½ cups water
¼ cup packed brown
  sugar
1 clove garlic, crushed

Sauce

½ cup chopped onion
1 clove garlic, crushed
1 tablespoon vegetable
  oil
425 g can tomato purée
2 tablespoons cider
  vinegar
1 tablespoon white sugar
1 tablespoon Mexican-
  style chilli powder, or
  to taste
1 teaspoon dried
  oregano
1 teaspoon ground
  cumin
bottled hot pepper sauce
  to taste

1 In large saucepan,
place spare ribs and bay
leaves. Combine water,
brown sugar and garlic;
pour over ribs.
2 Heat until boiling;
reduce heat and cover.
Gently simmer, turning
ribs occasionally, until
tender, about 30–45
minutes.
3 To make Sauce: in
small saucepan, cook
onion and garlic in oil
until soft. Stir in tomato
purée, vinegar, sugar,
chilli powder, oregano,
cumin and pepper sauce
to taste.
4 Heat until boiling;
reduce heat and simmer,
stirring occasionally, for
5 minutes. Cover and
keep warm
5 Drain ribs, pat dry on
paper towels. Grill
about 12 cm above
glowing coals, turning
and basting frequently
with sauce until
browned and glazed,
10–15 minutes. Serve
with remaining sauce.

Mustard Steaks

Preparation time:
  10 minutes
Cooking time:
  12 minutes
Serves 6

6 beef eye fillet steaks
¼ cup seeded mustard
2 tablespoons brandy
2 teaspoons olive oil
freshly ground black
  pepper

1 Trim any fat from
steaks. Combine
mustard, brandy, oil and
pepper and spread the
mixture evenly over each
steak.
2 Cook Mustard Steaks
over hot coals for 4–6
minutes each side for
medium rare meat.

Mustard Steaks and Mexican-style Beef Spare Ribs

Pork Cutlets Madras

Preparation time:
    30 minutes plus 1
    hour standing
Cooking time:
    10 minutes
Serves 6

6 pork cutlets, 3 cm
    thick
¼ cup apricot jam

¼ cup apricot juice
2 tablespoons white
    wine
1 tablespoon oil
1 tablespoon honey
2 teaspoons Madras
    curry powder
¼ teaspoon chilli
    powder

1 Trim pork cutlets of any excess fat. Combine apricot jam, juice, wine, oil, honey, curry powder and chilli; mix well.

2 Place pork cutlets in flat glass dish and pour over apricot mixture. Cover and stand for 1 hour at room temperature.

3 Drain, reserving marinade. Cook pork cutlets over glowing coals for about 10 minutes, turning once or twice and basting frequently with reserved marinade.

Ham Steaks with Mango Glaze and Pork Cutlets Madras

Ham Steaks with Mango Glaze

Preparation time:
  15 minutes
Cooking time:
  6 minutes
Serves 8

8 ham steaks, 1 cm thick
1 tablespoon oil
1 x 425 g can sliced mango
1 tablespoon orange juice
1 tablespoon butter, melted
1 tablespoon brown sugar
1 teaspoon grated fresh ginger
¼ teaspoon ground cloves

1 Using a small sharp knife score the edges of ham steaks at 5 cm intervals to prevent steaks curling. Brush ham steaks with oil.

2 Process or blend mango until smooth, add orange juice, butter, sugar, ginger and cloves, and process for about 30 seconds.
3 Cook ham steaks over glowing coals for about 2–3 minutes each side, basting frequently with mango glaze. Serve ham steaks immediately with any remaining mango glaze.

Barbecue Whole Fillet

Preparation time:
  20 minutes
Cooking time:
  30 minutes
Serves 8

1.5–2 kg whole tenderloin
2 tablespoons oil
1 clove garlic, crushed
freshly ground black pepper

1 Trim membrane, tendons and any excess fat from meat. Brush fillet with combined oil, garlic and pepper.
2 Barbecue whole over hot coals for about 30 minutes. Turn frequently, as this will allow the fillet to baste.
3 When cooked, carve into 1–2 cm slices starting at the thinner end, which will be well done. As you continue carving you will notice that the thicker portion of the fillet will be rarer — so, from one fillet, you can present well-done, medium, rare and blue beef.
4 Serve with horseradish or Béarnaise sauce or mustard. Slices of whole fillet look very attractive on thin slices of french bread.

Capricorn Lamb and Vegetables

Preparation time:
   8 minutes
Cooking time:
   16 minutes
Serves 4

8 *lean lamb chump chops*
4 *medium new potatoes, scrubbed*
4 *pieces pumpkin*
4 *medium zucchini, cut into 5 cm slices*
1 *tablespoon butter*
2 *tablespoons chopped chives*
1 *x 450 g can unsweetened pineapple slices, drained, juice reserved*
2 *tablespoons ginger marmalade*
¼ *teaspoon ground ginger*

1 Trim lamb chops of excess fat. Prick potatoes with a fork. Cook potatoes and pumpkin in water until only just tender.
2 Divide potatoes, pumpkin and zucchini between four squares of foil. Top each with a teaspoon of butter or margarine and sprinkle with chives. Wrap foil around vegetables to form a sealed package.
3 Barbecue chops and vegetable packages for 4–5 minutes. Combine 1 tablespoon reserved pineapple juice, marmalade and ground ginger. Turn chops, glaze with marmalade mixture. Turn vegetable packages and barbecue further 4–5 minutes. Continue to glaze chops.
4 Meanwhile, place pineapple slices on barbecue and brown each side. Serve chops with pineapple and vegetable packages.

HINT
When barbecuing foil-wrapped vegetable packages, you can slice vegetables for even cooking. Remember to open parcels carefully as hot steam escaping can burn.

Capricorn Lamb and Vegetables

Brazilian Beef Brochettes

Brazilian Beef Brochettes

Preparation time:
  18 minutes
Cooking time:
  12 minutes
Serves 4

750 g rump steak
1 tablespoon honey
1 tablespoon instant
  coffee powder
2 teaspoons lemon juice

2 cloves garlic, crushed
8 small green baby
  squash
8 small yellow baby
  squash
8 button mushrooms

1 Trim steak of any excess fat. Cut steak in 3 cm cubes. Marinate meat in combined honey, coffee powder, lemon juice and garlic for 10 minutes.
2 Thread meat onto 8 bamboo skewers, alternating with baby squash and mushrooms.
3 Barbecue brochettes over hot coals for 4–6 minutes each side or until cooked to taste.
4 Serve brochettes with salad vegetables and rice.

HINT
Soak bamboo skewers in cold water before use to prevent them burning while barbecuing.

15

Seasoned Pork Spare Ribs

Preparation time:
    40 minutes plus 4
    hours standing
Cooking time:
    15 minutes
Serves 8

1 kg pork spare ribs
1½ cups chicken stock
¼ cup soy sauce
2 tablespoons tomato
    sauce
1 tablespoon lemon juice
1 teaspoon chilli-and-
    garlic sauce

1 Simmer ribs in
chicken stock over low
heat for about 10
minutes. Remove from
heat; let ribs cool in the
stock. Drain ribs and
place in shallow dish.
2 Combine remaining
ingredients, brush over
ribs. Cover and chill for
3–4 hours.
3 Cook ribs about
15 cm above glowing
coals, turning and
basting often with
marinade until tender
and glazed, about 15
minutes.

HINT
Fresh pork is best
stored covered in the
coldest part of your
refrigerator for up to
three days.

Taco Pork Ribs

Preparation time:
    20 minutes
Cooking time:
    40 minutes
Serves 4

2 racks American-style
    pork spare ribs
⅔ cup tomato sauce
3 tablespoons taco sauce
    seasoning mix
3 cloves garlic, crushed
1 teaspoon honey
few drops red food
    colouring (optional)

1 In small bowl, stir
together tomato sauce,
taco sauce, garlic and
honey. Add food
colouring, if desired;
mix well. Brush mixture
over ribs.
2 Slowly cook ribs over
medium glowing coals,
turning frequently and
basting with glaze until
tender, 30–40 minutes.

Sherry Soy Pork Chops with Fruit

Preparation time:
    30 minutes plus 1
    hour standing
Cooking time:
    15 minutes
Serves 6

1 tablespoon chopped
    fresh marjoram or
    sage
2 tablespoons soy sauce
2 tablespoons sherry
1 clove garlic, crushed
6 pork loin chops
1 cup drained canned
    pineapple pieces
12 pitted dessert prunes

1 Combine first four
ingredients; mix well
and pour over chops in

shallow dish. Add pineapple and prunes. Cover and stand for 1 hour.

2 Drain, reserving the marinade. Thread fruit on to 1 or 2 skewers. Cook chops over medium glowing coals for 7 minutes, turning once or twice.

3 Place skewers on barbecue. Continue cooking, turning and basting occasionally with reserved marinade until pork is tender and fruit is heated through, about 7 minutes. Serve pork with fruit.

HINT

Pork is a delicate meat and it needs a gentle heat for barbecuing. Cook when the embers or coals have a gentle glow.

Clockwise from top: Seasoned Pork Spare Ribs, Taco Pork Ribs and Sherry Soy Pork Chops with Fruit

EXTRA SPECIAL BURGERS

Chicken and Herb Burger and Peppered Pork Burger

*O*ne of the easiest barbecued treats, loved by children and adults alike, hamburgers are fun to make and fun to eat. We give you six variations, each one delicious and different. Serve burgers either on a seeded bun with salad accompaniments or on a plate with salad, jacket potatoes and lots of tempting pickles, chutneys and relishes.

FOUR STEPS TO PERFECT BURGERS EVERY TIME

1 Divide mixture into even-sized portions.
2 Using wet hands, knead each portion until it holds together well. Flatten portions into rounds, about 2 cm thick.
3 Place on a baking tray and refrigerate for at least 30 minutes or until firm before barbecuing.
4 Barbecue burgers over glowing coals or embers, turning only once to avoid losing tasty juices.

Chicken and Herb Burgers

Preparation time:
    30 minutes plus 30
    minutes standing
Cooking time:
    10 minutes
Makes 8 burgers

500 g chicken thigh
    fillets
5 or 6 spring onions,
    finely chopped
1½ tablespoons
    chopped fresh thyme
1 egg, beaten
seasonings to taste

1 Chop chicken finely or place in a food processor and process until finely chopped.
2 Add remaining ingredients. Shape and chill.
3 Cook for 3–5 minutes each side. Serve garnished as desired.

Peppered Pork Burgers

Preparation time:
    30 minutes plus 30
    minutes standing
Cooking time:
    12 minutes
Makes 8 burgers

500 g lean pork
½ cup each finely
    chopped red and green
    capsicum
3 tablespoons corn
    kernels
1 cup fresh breadcrumbs
1 egg, beaten
seasonings to taste

1 Place pork in a food processor or blender. Process until finely chopped.
2 Combine pork with remaining ingredients in a bowl. Shape and chill.
3 Cook for 5–6 minutes each side. Serve garnished as desired.

HINT
Use a long-bladed spatula to slide burgers onto barbecue and to turn them.

Beef Burgers

Preparation time:
    30 minutes plus 30
    minutes standing time
Cooking time:
    10 minutes
Makes 8 burgers

1 kg lean minced steak
2 onions, finely chopped
1 egg, beaten
2 cloves garlic, crushed
1 tablespoon chilli sauce
2 teaspoons garam
    masala
seasonings to taste

1 Combine all ingredients well with your hands. Shape and chill.
2 Cook for 3–5 minutes each side. Serve garnished as desired.

Cheese and Bacon Burgers

Preparation time:
  30 minutes plus 30
  minutes standing
Cooking time:
  12 minutes
Makes 8 burgers

500 g rindless bacon,
  chopped
250 g lean pork,
  trimmed and chopped
½ cup shredded
  Cheddar cheese
¼ cup grated Parmesan
  cheese
½ cup fresh
  breadcrumbs

pinch cayenne pepper
seasonings to taste

1 Place bacon, pork,
cheeses, breadcrumbs
and seasonings in a food
processor or blender.
Process until finely
chopped. Shape the
mixture and chill.

Cheese and Bacon Burger

2 Cook for 6 minutes each side. Serve on wholegrain bread or bun, garnished as desired.

HINT
Cooked white or brown rice may be substituted for fresh breadcrumbs in this burger recipe. The result will have a moist texture.

Bean Burgers

Preparation time:
   30 minutes plus 30 minutes standing time
Cooking time:
   12 minutes
Makes 8 burgers

1 x 300 g *can kidney beans, drained*
1 *onion, chopped*
1 *carrot, chopped*
2 *tablespoons toasted sesame seeds*
1 *clove garlic, crushed*
2 *tablespoons tomato paste or sauce*
1 *cup fresh breadcrumbs*
½ *teaspoon Tabasco sauce*
seasonings to taste
1 *egg, beaten*

1 Place all ingredients except egg in a food processor or blender. Process until finely chopped.
2 Add enough egg to bind the mixture. Shape and chill.
3 Cook for 5–6 minutes each side. Serve garnished as desired.

Spiced Lamb Burgers

Preparation time:
   30 minutes plus 30 minutes standing
Cooking time:
   10 minutes
Makes 8 burgers

500 g *minced lamb*
1 *cup fresh breadcrumbs*
⅓ *cup sultanas*
2 *teaspoons cinnamon*
2 *teaspoons ground coriander*
1 *teaspoon chopped fresh rosemary (or ¼ teaspoon dried)*
1 *egg, beaten*

1 Combine all ingredients well. Shape and chill.
2 Cook for 3–5 minutes each side. Serve garnished as desired.

HINT
If you can't get minced lamb, buy some lamb chops, trim and remove bones and chop finely in the food processor.

SUCCULENT SEAFOOD AND POULTRY

Chicken Breasts with Cumin and Lime and Garlic and Chilli Prawns

Seafood and poultry are naturally tender and delectable, even more so when they are barbecued over glowing coals.

Seafood requires gentle short barbecuing. You can use whole fresh fish, cutlets or fillets. Whole fish may be cooked in a hinged wire basket or wrapped in heavy-duty foil. Cutlets and fillets may be cooked directly over an oiled grill or barbecue plate, or they may also be wrapped in foil. Baste and turn fish two or three times during cooking.

Poultry of all types is ideal to barbecue. Chicken pieces, wings and drumsticks are always popular and economical too. Whole spatchcocks are best when they have their backbones removed and are flattened for even cooking. Duck and quail can also be successfully barbecued. To introduce flavour and to moisten birds, marinate them overnight and baste them frequently with marinade or flavoured oils.

Chicken Breasts with Cumin and Lime

Preparation time:
  20 minutes
Cooking time:
  16 minutes
Serves 6

6 boneless chicken
  breasts
1 teaspoon ground
  cumin
juice of 1 or 2 limes
freshly ground pepper
vegetable oil

1 Remove skin from chicken if desired. Sprinkle with cumin, lime juice and pepper.
2 Grill over medium-hot coals until chicken is tender (lightly baste skinless chicken with oil to prevent scorching),

about 5–8 minutes each side.
3 Serve with lime-flavoured butter.

> **HINT**
> Basting chicken breasts with a flavoured oil adds tang and keeps chicken moist.

> **HINT**
> A quick and tasty baste for barbecued prawns can be made from equal quantities of bottled soy sauce, teriyaki sauce and lemon juice.

Garlic and Chilli Prawns

Preparation time:
  40 minutes plus
  overnight standing
Cooking time:
  4 minutes
Serves 4

750 g green king prawns
¾ cup olive oil
4 cloves garlic, crushed
½ tablespoon bottled
  chilli sauce (optional)
½ tablespoon grated
  lemon rind
1 teaspoon sugar
½ teaspoon cracked
  black pepper

1 Peel and devein prawns, leaving the tail intact. Place prawns in a glass bowl.
2 Combine oil, garlic, chilli sauce, lemon rind, sugar and pepper and mix well. Pour over prawns, stirring to coat them evenly. Cover and refrigerate overnight.
3 Cook prawns on a well-oiled barbecue plate for 3–4 minutes, brushing with marinade continuously during cooking. Take care not to overcook.

Barbecued Fish Fillets

Preparation time:
20 minutes plus 30 minutes standing
Cooking time:
6 minutes
Serves 4

4 *medium-sized white fish fillets*
2 *tablespoons lemon juice*
1 *tablespoon olive oil*
1 *small white onion, finely chopped*
1 *tablespoon chopped parsley*
1 *tablespoon Pernod*
freshly ground black pepper

1 Place fish fillets in flat glass dish. Combine juice, oil, onion, parsley, Pernod and pepper and pour over fillets. Stand covered for 30 minutes.
2 Cook fish fillets on a barbecue plate, brushing with oil for 3 minutes each side.
3 Serve Barbecued Fish Fillets with lemon

Madrid-Style Cod Cutlets and Barbecued Fish Fillets

wedges, parsley and basil mayonnaise.

Madrid-Style Cod Cutlets

Preparation time:
   30 minutes plus 2
   hours standing
Cooking time:
   8 minutes
Serves 6

6 cod cutlets

Marinade
⅔ cup orange juice
⅓ cup lime juice
2 tablespoons olive oil
2 cloves garlic, crushed
1 tablespoon green
   peppercorns, crushed
½ teaspoon dried
   oregano leaves
¼ teaspoon ground
   cumin

1 Combine citrus juices, oil, garlic, peppercorns, oregano and cumin thoroughly.

2 Place cutlets in a flat glass dish, pour marinade over, cover and stand for several hours.
3 Cook cutlets on a well-greased barbecue for 3–4 minutes each side, basting frequently with marinade. Serve cutlets with lime wedges.

Chilli Fish Parcels

Preparation time:
   20 minutes
Cooking time:
   10 minutes
Serves 4

4 boneless fish fillets
2–3 teaspoons chopped
   chilli
1 onion, thinly sliced
2 tomatoes, thinly sliced
juice of 1 lemon
1 tablespoon olive oil
1 tablespoon chopped
   parsley
seasonings to taste

1 Place each fish fillet in a square of aluminium foil. Spread fish with chilli.
2 Top with onion rings and tomato. Sprinkle with lemon juice, oil, parsley and seasonings.
3 Wrap each fillet tightly in foil. Place on barbecue plate or over grill and cook for 10–15 minutes or until fish flakes easily when tested with a fork.
Note. Two tablespoons of white wine may be substituted for the lemon juice.

Chilli Fish Parcels

25

Sweet-and-Sour Barbecued Chicken Wings

Preparation time:
    30 minutes plus 1
    hour standing
Cooking time:
    45 minutes
Serves 10

1.5 kg chicken wings
1 cup apricot jam
2 tablespoons white
    vinegar
1 tablespoon soy sauce
1 tablespoon tomato
    sauce
1 tablespoon oil
1 clove garlic, crushed

1 Remove wing tips
from chicken and trim
away excess fat.
2 Stir apricot jam,
vinegar, soy sauce,
tomato sauce, oil and
garlic in a small
saucepan over a low heat
until combined. Pour
over chicken wings and
mix well. Cover and
stand for 1 hour.
3 Drain excess marinade
from chicken wings.
Place wings in a large
baking tray and cook in
a moderate oven
(180°C) for 30 minutes
(you may need to add ½
cup water to the baking
tray to prevent wings
sticking). Turn wings
halfway through
cooking.
4 Take wings out of
baking tray and continue

cooking over hot coals
for 10–15 minutes,
brushing with oil if
necessary.

HINT
Chicken wings can be
served as a main
course dish or as tasty
appetisers. Supply
guests with lots of
napkins and a small
bowl for chicken
bones.

Orange-Glazed Chicken Drumsticks

Preparation time:
    20 minutes
Cooking time:
    35 minutes
Serves 6

12 chicken drumsticks
3 tablespoons
    marmalade
1 tablespoon orange
    juice
1 tablespoon seeded
    mustard
1 tablespoon lemon juice
1 teaspoon ground
    coriander

1 Stir together
marmalade, orange
juice, mustard, lemon
juice and coriander.
2 Lightly oil barbecue
grill, place drumsticks
over grill and brush each
lightly with orange

glaze. Cook chicken for
about 30–35 minutes or
until cooked when tested
with a skewer. Baste
drumsticks with glaze
while cooking, taking
care not to brown them
too quickly.

Ginger Spice Chicken Kebabs

Preparation time:
    30 minutes plus 2
    hours standing
Cooking time:
    15 minutes
Serves 6

750 g boneless chicken
    thighs
½ cup white wine
1 tablespoon honey
1 tablespoon sesame oil
1 tablespoon grated
    fresh ginger
¼ teaspoon Chinese
    five-spice powder
¼ teaspoon chilli
    powder

1 Cut chicken into 3 cm
cubes. Thread chicken
evenly onto 12 skewers.
2 Combine wine,
honey, sesame oil,
ginger, five-spice and
chilli. Pour over chicken
skewers, cover and
refrigerate for several
hours or overnight.
3 Cook chicken over
hot coals for 10–15
minutes, turning
frequently and brushing
with oil when necessary.

Sweet-and-Sour Chicken Wings, Orange-Glazed Chicken Drumsticks and Ginger Spice Chicken Kebabs

Sweet and Spicy Spatchcocks

Preparation time:
40 minutes plus 24 hours standing
Cooking time:
30 minutes
Serves 8

4 spatchcocks, halved
and cleaned

Marinade

1 x 825 g can plums,
drained and stoned
1 onion, roughly
chopped
2 cloves garlic, crushed
¼ cup red wine
¼ cup teriyaki sauce
2 tablespoons chilli
sauce
juice of 1 lemon
1 teaspoon sesame oil
freshly ground pepper

1 Make 3 or 4 deep slashes in the flesh of each half spatchcock. Set aside.
2 To prepare Marinade: place all ingredients in a food processor or blender. Process until smooth.
3 Place spatchcocks skin side down in a shallow ovenproof dish. Pour over marinade. Turn spatchcocks to ensure they are well coated. Cover. Marinate in the refrigerator, turning and basting frequently, for at least 24 hours.
4 Drain spatchcock. Cook over hot coals for 15 minutes each side, basting frequently with marinade.

HINT
Spatchcocks are small chickens which are available in speciality chicken shops. Spatchcocks should be halved lengthwise by cutting through the backbone.

Sweet and Spicy Spatchcocks

Sweet and Spicy Salmon Cutlets

Sweet and Spicy Salmon Cutlets

Preparation time:
  30 minutes plus 3
  hours standing
Cooking time:
  4 minutes
Serves 6

6 salmon cutlets
rind and juice of 2 limes
2 tablespoons honey
2 tablespoons soy sauce
1 tablespoon chilli sauce

2 tablespoons prepared
  grain mustard
½ teaspoon sesame oil
freshly ground black
  pepper

1 Combine all
ingredients except
salmon in a shallow
dish. Add salmon. Turn
to coat both sides.
2 Cover with plastic
wrap. Marinate in the
refrigerator for 2–3
hours, basting
frequently.
3 Barbecue for 2
minutes each side,

basting from time to
time. Serve salmon with
extra soy, lime juice and
sesame oil if desired.

HINT
Salmon is a very
delicate fish and
needs gentle cooking.
Do not overcook it; it
should be a little
darker in the middle.
Check by making a
small cut in the
centre.

BARBECUE KETTLE COOKERY

Barbecued Ginger Pork Loin

*B*arbecue kettles have become very popular in recent years. When meat, poultry and seafood are cooked in a barbecue kettle they have an excellent flavour and appearance and they retain their natural juices. The secret of this style of cooking lies in the design of these round barbecues, enabling you not only to grill but also to roast and bake large pieces of meat, whole joints, vegetables and even desserts.

The recipes we have given you for the barbecue kettle all call for a normal fire with indirect heat. To obtain this the food is placed on the upper grill between two fires directly over a foil tray.

We suggest you refer to your own barbecue kettle manual before beginning these recipes.

Barbecued Ginger Pork Loin

Preparation time:
 40 minutes plus
 overnight standing
Cooking time:
 2 hours
Serves 8

2 tablespoons finely
 chopped fresh thyme
1 tablespoon Dijon
 mustard
2.5 kg boneless rolled
 loin pork roast
½ cup green ginger wine
 or dry sherry or white
 wine
½ cup soy sauce
½ cup vegetable oil
2 large cloves garlic,
 crushed
watercress to garnish

1 Stir together thyme and mustard; rub paste all over rolled pork. Place in shallow baking dish.

2 Combine ginger wine, soy sauce, oil and garlic; pour over pork. Cover and refrigerate overnight, turning pork occasionally to marinate.
3 One hour before cooking, let pork stand in marinade at room temperature. Remove pork from marinade; pat dry on paper towels. Reserve the marinade.
4 Place pork on rack over tray. Sear, turning every 15 minutes, until browned all over. Raise rack to highest position above coals. Cover with domed lid.
5 Continue cooking, turning and brushing frequently with marinade, until pork is tender and juices run clear when pierced, 1–1½ hours.
6 Let the roast stand on a cutting board, covered with foil, for 10 minutes, Remove string;

carve into thin slices. Garnish with watercress.

Barbecued Sausages

Preparation time:
 20 minutes
Cooking time:
 20 minutes
Makes 1 kg

1 kg pork sausages

Glaze
½ cup brown sugar
1 teaspoon seeded
 mustard
2 tablespoons tomato
 sauce

1 Place the sausages on the barbecue and put the lid on. Cook thick sausages for 15–20 minutes and thin sausages for 10–15 minutes.
2 To glaze the sausages, combine the brown sugar, mustard and tomato sauce. Heat in a saucepan until sugar has dissolved. Brush the sausages with this glaze occasionally while they are cooking.

Barbecued Beef with Lemon and Mustard Butter

Preparation time:
   20 minutes
Cooking time:
   40 minutes
Serves 6

1 kg piece beef
olive oil
3 cloves garlic, crushed
2 tablespoons cracked
   black peppercorns

1   Trim beef of excess fat and brush with olive oil and garlic. Spread peppercorns evenly over barbecued beef.
2   Place beef on a rack over a tray. Cover with lid and cook for 40 minutes for medium doneness.
3   Stand 10 minutes before slicing. Serve with Lemon and Mustard Butter.

Lemon and Mustard Butter

125 g butter
2 tablespoons chopped
   parsley
1 tablespoon seeded
   mustard
1 tablespoon lemon juice
1 tablespoon grated
   lemon rind

Beat the parsley and butter together; add the mustard, lemon juice and rind and beat in. Form this mixture into a roll. Slice butter in 1 cm slices and serve over barbecued beef.

Barbecued Beef with Lemon and Mustard Butter

Grilled Chicken with Chilli and Coriander

Grilled Chicken with Chilli and Coriander

Preparation time:
20 minutes plus 1½ hours standing
Cooking time:
50 minutes
Serves 4

1 kg chicken Maryland pieces

Marinade
½ cup soy sauce
2 tablespoons lemon juice
2 tablespoons honey
1 tablespoon sesame oil
3 small fresh chillies, finely chopped
2 tablespoons finely chopped coriander

1 Combine soy sauce, lemon juice, honey, sesame oil, chilli and coriander in a large bowl and mix well. Add the chicken pieces, turning them to coat them. Marinate the chicken, covered, in the refrigerator for 1½ hours.
2 Remove the chicken pieces from the marinade and place them on the barbecue. Cook with lid on for 45–50 minutes.
3 Serve with extra soy sauce and chopped chilli and coriander.

33

Baked Whole Fish with Garlic and Herbs

Baked Whole Fish with Garlic and Herbs

Preparation time:
   20 minutes
Cooking time:
   50 minutes
Serves 4

1 *whole fish, about*
   2.5 kg
60 *g butter, melted*
2 *cloves garlic, crushed*
2 *tablespoons chopped*
   fresh herbs
lemon juice
freshly ground black
   pepper

1 Wash and scale the fish. Place the fish upright on a sheet of oiled foil, formed into a tray, with its body curved and its fins used to prop it up. Brush it with combined butter, garlic and herbs and squeeze lemon juice over it. Season with pepper. Enclose fish securely in foil.
2 Cook it on the barbecue with the lid on, for 40–50 minutes.

HINT
Avoid salting meats before barbecuing as the salt brings the juices of the meat to the surface. The result is tough, dry meat.

Leg of Lamb with Rosemary and Garlic

Preparation time:
   20 minutes
Cooking time:
   1¾ hours
Serves 8

1.5 *kg leg of lamb*
olive oil
2 *cloves garlic, cut in*
   small pieces
2 *tablespoons rosemary*
freshly ground black
   pepper

Brush the lamb with oil. Make small slits over lamb and insert garlic and rosemary; sprinkle with pepper. Place the lamb on a rack over a tray. Cover with lid and cook for 1½–1¾ hours, or until done.

Leg of Lamb with Rosemary and Garlic

MARINADES, BASTES AND RELISHES

Clockwise from top left: Honey and Ginger Baste, Herb-flavoured Oil, Lime and Dill Marinade, Spiced Chutney Glaze and Quick Cupboard Marinade

*B*arbecued meats previously marinated have an exciting and unexpected flavour. Choose any meat — beef, lamb, pork, chicken or game — and create a different combination with each marinade you use. As a rule marinades are best made 24 hours ahead to enhance flavours, and the longer the meat is kept in the marinade the more effective it will be. The usual length of time is overnight, which produces a tasty and tender result.

Equal quantities of oil and an acid such as wine or lemon juice make a good base. The oil helps preserve moisture while the acid tenderises the meat. To this base add flavourings: crushed garlic, spices, herbs like oregano, rosemary or basil are ideal. Add a generous dash of bottled teriyaki or soy sauce, Worcestershire sauce or mustard. Never be strict with yourself — find new combinations. Honey and citrus go well with chicken, duck or quail, and pork is delicious with a marinade of soy sauce, brown sugar and freshly grated ginger.

When barbecuing tender cuts of meat or seafood a tasty basting mixture may be all you need to flavour and moisten meats directly on the barbecue. Bastes can be made quickly and brushed over foods while barbecuing. They can be as simple as flavoured oils and vinegars or they can be mixtures of flavourings such as honey, brown sugar, citrus juice, marmalade and spices.

We have also included some favourite relishes, mustards and sauces to serve along with your barbecued meats. These zesty accompaniments complement smoky-flavoured meats, seafood and poultry beautifully. Flavoured butters provide a simple garnish and a delightfully moist flavoured dressing as they slowly melt over barbecued meats.

Quick Cupboard Marinade

Use this marinade for any red meats.

Preparation time:
  10 minutes
Cooking time:
  nil
Makes 1¼ cups

½ cup oil
½ cup red wine
2 tablespoons barbecue
  sauce
2 tablespoons tomato
  sauce
1 teaspoon
  Worcestershire sauce
1 teaspoon chilli sauce
½ teaspoon ground
  black pepper

Combine all ingredients thoroughly.

Lime and Dill Marinade

This marinade is ideal to use with quail or chicken.

Preparation time:
  10 minutes
Cooking time:
  nil
Makes 1¼ cups

½ cup olive oil
½ cup lime juice
¼ cup white wine
2 tablespoons finely
  chopped dill
2 teaspoons sugar
2 teaspoons sesame oil

Combine all ingredients thoroughly.

Honey and Ginger Baste

Brush this baste over pork, chicken or lamb.

Preparation time:
  10 minutes
Cooking time:
  nil
Makes 1½ cups

½ cup pineapple juice
½ cup orange juice
¼ cup honey
2 tablespoons oil
1 tablespoon grated
  fresh ginger

Combine all ingredients thoroughly. Brush over meat while barbecuing.

Flavoured Oils

Preparation time:
  10 minutes plus 5 days
  standing
Cooking time:
  2 minutes
Makes 2 cups

2 cups vegetable oil
10–12 tablespoons
  chopped fresh herbs
  (see Note)
sprigs of fresh herbs

1 Heat oil in a double saucepan (to prevent oil breaking down). Add herbs. Remove from heat. Allow to stand for 5 days.
2 Strain into a sterilised bottle. Add a fresh sprig of herb. Seal. Store in a cool place.
Note. Use basil, garlic or sage for your oils or experiment with other herbs of your choice.

> **HINT**
> This flavoured oil can also be used as the base oil in a vinaigrette dressing.

Spiced Chutney Glaze

This baste is delicious with lamb or pork.

Preparation time:
  10 minutes

Cooking time:
  nil
Makes 1½ cups

½ cup fruit chutney
¼ cup melted butter
¼ cup lemon juice
¼ cup water
2 teaspoons curry
  powder
½ teaspoon ground
  ginger
½ teaspoon cinnamon

Combine all ingredients thoroughly. Brush over meat while barbecuing.

> **HINT**
> Keep the baste mixture in a small jug to make basting easy. Brush food at regular intervals while barbecuing to moisten and flavour evenly.

Honey and Soy Marinade

This marinade is ideal for pork. Try adding 2 teaspoons of sesame oil.

Preparation time:
  10 minutes
Cooking time:
  nil
Makes 1½ cups

½ cup honey
½ cup white wine
¼ cup soy sauce
¼ cup oil
2 cloves garlic, crushed
seasonings to taste

Combine all ingredients thoroughly.

> **HINT**
> For ease of measuring honey, heat the measuring jug with hot water and have the honey at room temperature.

Lemon and Garlic Marinade

This marinade is excellent for chicken or fish.

Preparation time:
  10 minutes
Cooking time:
  nil
Makes 1½ cups

juice and rind of 6
  lemons
½ cup white wine
½ cup oil
4 cloves garlic, crushed
½ cup chopped fresh
  parsley
seasonings to taste

Combine all ingredients thoroughly.

Herb Butters

Herb Butter

Preparation time:
  30 minutes
Cooking time:
  nil
Makes 15 slices

125 g butter, at room
  temperature
3 tablespoons chopped
  fresh herb (e.g.,
  tarragon, chives,
  basil, parsley, dill,
  oregano) or 2
  teaspoons dried herb
1 tablespoon finely
  chopped onion
1 tablespoon lemon juice
freshly ground black
  pepper

1 Beat all ingredients
together in a small bowl.
2 Form mixture into a
15 cm log on a sheet of
aluminium foil. Wrap up
tightly. Twist ends of
foil to compress butter.
3 Place in the freezer to
store (for up to 2
months).
4 Cut into 1 cm slices to
serve. Place a pat on
grilled meat, fish or
chicken.

HINT
Herb butter may also
be served in a butter
pat, with guests
helping themselves.
This tasty spread can
accompany
barbecued meats,
seafood, potatoes and
bread.

39

Orange and Redcurrant Baste

Use this baste over duck, chicken or pork.

Preparation time:
  10 minutes
Cooking time:
  nil
Makes 1½ cups

½ cup orange juice
½ cup redcurrant jelly
2 tablespoons sherry
2 tablespoons soy sauce
1 tablespoon brown
  sugar

Combine all ingredients thoroughly. Brush over meat while barbecuing.

Redcurrant Mustard Relish

Preparation time:
  15 minutes
Cooking time:
  nil
Makes 1 cup

⅔ cup seeded mustard
⅓ cup redcurrant jelly
2 teaspoons horseradish
  relish

Place all ingredients in a blender and whizz together, or combine thoroughly by hand.

Herb Mustard

Preparation time:
  20 minutes
Cooking time:
  nil
Makes 2 cups

¼ cup white mustard
  seeds
1 cup blanched almonds
1 cup oil
1 cup white vinegar
¼ cup sherry
1 tablespoon chopped
  fresh chives
1 tablespoon chopped
  fresh parsley
1 tablespoon chopped
  fresh dill

1 Place mustard seeds and almonds in a food processor. Process until well ground.
2 Combine all remaining ingredients. Gradually pour through chute with motor running. Process until thick and creamy.
3 Spoon into sterilised jars. Seal and store in a cool place.

HINT
Any combination of fresh herbs may be used in this recipe.

Hot Grain Mustard

Preparation time:
  40 minutes
Cooking time:
  nil
Makes 3 cups

½ cup black mustard
  seeds
½ cup yellow mustard
  seeds
1 teaspoon black
  peppercorns, lightly
  crushed
1 cup oil
1 cup white vinegar
1 cup white wine
2 teaspoons chopped
  fresh herbs of choice
2 egg yolks, beaten

1 Combine all ingredients except the beaten egg yolks in a medium-sized bowl. Mix well.
2 Place bowl over a saucepan of simmering water. Gradually whisk in egg yolks. Continue whisking until mixture is thick and creamy.
3 Spoon into sterilised jars. Seal and store in a cool place.

HINTS
☐ Mustard seeds are available from speciality Asian stores and health food stores.
☐ Store all spice in airtight containers in a cool dark place.

Hot Grain Mustard, Herb Mustard and Redcurrant Mustard Relish

Fresh Apricot Relish

Preparation time:
  40 minutes
Cooking time:
  40 minutes
Makes 5 cups

1 kg fresh apricots,
  halved and pitted
375 g onions, chopped
2 cups packed brown
  sugar

1 ½ cups raisins
1 ½ cups cider vinegar
¼ cup chopped
  preserved ginger
1 tablespoon white
  mustard seeds
2 small red chillies, seeds
  removed and finely
  chopped
2 teaspoons salt
½ teaspoon cinnamon

1 Chop apricots into small pieces and place in large heavy-based saucepan with all remaining ingredients. Stir over moderate heat until sugar is dissolved.
2 Heat until boiling; reduce heat. Simmer, uncovered, until mixture is thick and pulpy, stirring occasionally, about 40 minutes.
3 Spoon into warm, sterilised jars; seal and store in a cool, dry dark place. Refrigerate after opening.

41

SALADS AND VEGETABLES

*Clockwise from top: Spring Slaw, Spinach and Bacon Salad
and Marinated Zucchini and Tomato with Mint*

*N*o barbecue is ever complete without a salad. Ingredients may be simple or exotic but they must always be the freshest seasonal best. Most salad ingredients can be prepared in advance, but it is best to assemble and dress a salad just before serving. A green leafy salad, dressed with fresh herbs and a good quality oil and vinegar just before serving time, cannot be surpassed. You will then need to serve only one or two other salads, the choice of which is up to you, but remember to take into account the flavours, colours and texture of the rest of your barbecue menu.

Vegetables lend themselves to barbecue cookery beautifully. They need little preparation — only a light brush with oil and then on to the barbecue plate or grill. Remember to baste them frequently with oil or a combination of soy sauce, lemon juice and herbs. You may also wrap vegetables in heavy duty aluminium foil. Drizzle them with melted butter and garlic and wrap them securely, leaving room for steam expansion. Remember to take care when unwrapping them. Do not overcook vegetables: to be at their best they should be just tender.

Spinach and Bacon Salad

Preparation time:
   30 minutes
Cooking time:
   nil
Serves 8

6 rashers rindless bacon, chopped
1 bunch spinach, stems removed and torn into bite-sized pieces
½ small bunch of watercress, broken into sprigs
1 onion, sliced
125 g mushrooms, sliced
1 quantity Vinaigrette Dressing (see Step-by-Step recipe)

1 Place bacon in a dry frying pan. Cook over a medium heat until crisp. Drain. Set aside.
2 Arrange spinach, watercress, onion and mushrooms in a serving bowl. Top with bacon and dressing just before serving. Toss well.

Marinated Zucchini and Tomato with Mint

Preparation time:
   40 minutes plus overnight standing
Cooking time:
   nil
Serves 10

1 kg zucchini, trimmed
4 medium sized tomatoes
½ cup olive oil
2 cloves garlic, finely chopped
2 tablespoons coarsely chopped fresh mint
½ teaspoon salt
freshly ground pepper
½ cup white wine vinegar

1 Cut zucchini into rounds, about 5 mm thick.
2 Heat oil in large frying pan. Cook zucchini in batches, one layer deep, until golden on both sides, about 3 minutes. Transfer with slotted spoon to a serving bowl.
3 Slice tomatoes and place over zucchini in serving bowl. Sprinkle with garlic, mint, salt and pepper to taste.
4 Heat vinegar until boiling and pour over zucchini and tomatoes.
5 Cover and chill at least overnight, gently stirring once or twice, before serving.

HINT
This recipe can be prepared several days in advance and makes a delicious accompaniment to all barbecued or roast meats and poultry.

43

Spring Slaw

Preparation time:
  40 minutes
Cooking time:
  nil
Serves 8

6 cups shredded green
  cabbage
2 oranges, peeled,
  seeded and sectioned
1 large red apple, cored
  and diced
1 each small green and
  red capsicum, seeded,
  cut into julienne strips
½ cup mayonnaise
½ cup low-fat yoghurt
½ teaspoon celery seeds
freshly ground pepper

1 In serving bowl, toss
together cabbage,
orange, apple, green and
red capsicum. Cover;
chill until needed.
2 Stir together
mayonnaise, yoghurt
and celery seeds,
seasoning to taste with
pepper. Cover and chill.
3 Just before serving,
pour dressing over salad;
toss well.

Classic Green Salad

Classic Green Salad

Preparation time:
  30 minutes plus
  overnight standing
Cooking time:
  nil
Serves 10

1 butterhead or cabbage
  lettuce
1 small cos lettuce
1 cup packed torn young
  spinach leaves
1 cup vegetable oil
½ cup red wine vinegar
3 cloves garlic, crushed
2 tablespoons chopped
  fresh thyme or
  marjoram leaves
2 tablespoons finely
  chopped parsley
½ teaspoon salt
freshly ground pepper
1 cup sliced button
  mushrooms
1 cup crisp-cooked
  broccoli florets

1 medium Spanish (red)
  onion, thinly sliced
  into rings
2 small tomatoes, cut in
  thin wedges
grated Parmesan cheese
  (optional)

1 Wash and dry lettuces
and spinach leaves. Pack
in a large plastic bag;
chill thoroughly until
crisp.
2 Place oil and next five
ingredients in large
container with tight-
fitting lid. Add plenty of
pepper. Cover; shake
vigorously until blended.
Let stand at least
overnight to blend
flavours.
3 To serve, arrange
greens, mushrooms,
broccoli, onion and
tomatoes in serving
bowl. Drizzle with
dressing to taste and toss
to coat well. Sprinkle
with Parmesan if
desired.

Step-by-Step to Vinaigrette Dressing

Preparation time:
  15 minutes
Cooking time:
  nil
Makes 1 cup

¹/₃ cup vinegar
1 clove garlic, crushed
2 teaspoons Dijon
  mustard (see Note)
salt and freshly ground
  black pepper to taste

¹/₂ cup vegetable oil
¹/₂ cup olive oil

1 To make Vinaigrette by hand: whisk vinegar, garlic, mustard, salt and pepper together in a small bowl until well blended.

2 Gradually whisk oil into the vinegar mixture until Vinaigrette is well blended and smooth. Use immediately or refrigerate. Whisk before using.

3 To prepare Vinaigrette in a screw-top jar: place all ingredients in jar. Cover. Shake until well blended.

4 To prepare Vinaigrette in a food processor: place vinegar, garlic, mustard, salt and pepper in bowl. Process for 2–3 seconds. Gradually pour oil through chute while machine is running. Process for 2–3 seconds.
Note. Any prepared mustard may be used in place of Dijon.

Step 1

Step 2

Step 3

Step 4

Asparagus and Snow Pea Salad

Preparation time:
  30 minutes
Cooking time:
  nil
Serves 8

200 g *fresh snow peas or*
  sugar snap peas
2 *bunches fresh*
  asparagus
2 *cos lettuces, washed*
  and dried
1 *punnet cherry*
  tomatoes
1 *avocado, peeled,*
  pitted and sliced

Dressing

½ *teaspoon grated*
  orange rind
½ *cup fresh orange juice*
1 *tablespoon toasted*
  sesame seeds
2 *tablespoons olive oil*
2 *teaspoons honey*
1 *teaspoon soy sauce*
few drops sesame oil

1 To make salad: trim and blanch snow peas in boiling water for 30 seconds; refresh under cold water and drain.
2 Trim and cut asparagus into desired lengths. Cook in simmering water, covered, until crisp tender, 3–4 minutes. Refresh and drain; chill.
3 Line a salad bowl with some of the lettuce leaves. Add remaining lettuce (torn into pieces), the snow peas, asparagus, tomatoes and avocado. Cover and chill until needed (if storing for a long time, dip avocado slices in lemon juice).
4 To make dressing: in small container with tight-fitting lid, combine orange rind and juice, sesame seeds, olive oil, honey, soy sauce and sesame oil to taste. Cover and shake well.
5 To serve, pour dressing over salad; toss.

> HINT
> Asparagus is very perishable. Decay generally starts at the tip of the spear. To store, wrap asparagus with damp absorbent paper, place in a plastic bag and keep in the vegetable crisper.

Hot Minted Potato Salad

Preparation time:
  30 minutes
Cooking time:
  18 minutes
Serves 8

1 kg *tiny new potatoes*
5 *large sprigs of fresh*
  mint
1 *cup sour light cream*
2 *tablespoons*
  mayonnaise
1 *medium white onion,*
  grated
¼ *cup chopped parsley*
2 *tablespoons chopped*
  fresh dill
2 *tablespoons chopped*
  chives
salt and ground pepper

1 Place potatoes and mint in large saucepan; add enough water to cover. Heat until boiling; reduce heat and cover. Gently simmer until potatoes are just tender, about 10–12 minutes. Drain well; discard mint.
2 In bowl, stir together sour cream, mayonnaise, onion, fresh herbs and seasonings to taste. Add to hot potatoes and mix well. Serve warm.

> HINT
> Small new potatoes have a waxy firm quality which is ideal for boiling and serving hot with butter and pepper or dressed with light creamy dressings.

Hot Minted Potato Salad and Asparagus and Snow Pea Salad

Savoury Jacket Potatoes

Preparation time:
    40 minutes
Cooking time:
    1½ hours
Serves 8

8 medium potatoes,
    scrubbed

Chilli con Carne
    Topping

1 tablespoon oil
30 g butter
1 onion, chopped
250 g minced steak
*1 tablespoon tomato
    paste*
1 x 425 g can tomatoes
*½ cup drained canned
    red kidney beans*
1 tablespoon chilli sauce
1 teaspoon chilli powder
few drops Tabasco sauce
seasonings to taste

Cheese and Avocado
    Topping

30 g butter
1 tablespoon flour
1 cup milk
pinch cayenne pepper
seasonings to taste
*1 cup shredded Cheddar
    cheese*
1 avocado, sliced

Spicy Mushroom
    Topping

60 g butter
1 onion, chopped
1 clove garlic, crushed
500 g mushrooms, sliced
*2 tablespoons chilli
    sauce*

*1 teaspoon chilli powder
seasonings to taste
300 mL carton cream*

1 Prick each potato well
all over with a fork.
Place on a baking tray.
Bake in a moderate oven
(180°C) for 1½ hours or
until crisp on the outside
and tender inside.
2 To prepare Chilli con
Carne Topping: heat oil
and butter together in a
large frying pan. Cook
onion until tender.
3 Add mince. Brown
well. Blend in remaining
ingredients. Cover.
Simmer for 25–30
minutes. Cut open jacket
potatoes. Spoon over
filling. Serve with a
dollop of sour cream, if
desired.
4 To prepare Cheese
and Avocado Topping:
melt butter in a small
saucepan. Add flour.
Mix well. Cook 1
minute.

5 Remove from heat.
Gradually blend in milk.
Return to heat. Cook,
stirring constantly, until
sauce boils and thickens.
Simmer for 3 minutes.
Stir in the seasonings
and half of the cheese.
6 Cut open jacket
potatoes. Insert slices of
avocado. Spoon over
sauce. Sprinkle with
leftover cheese. Grill
until cheese is melted
and golden.
7 To prepare Spicy
Mushroom Topping:
melt butter in a large
frying pan. Cook onion
and garlic until onion is
tender. Add
mushrooms, chilli sauce,
chilli powder and
seasonings. Cook 10
minutes.
8 Pour over cream.
Simmer for 10 minutes
or until thickened. Cut
open jacket potatoes.
Pour over mushroom
sauce.

Savoury Jacket Potatoes

Beetroot Shreds with Two Sauces

Beetroot Shreds with Two Sauces

Preparation time:
  40 minutes
Cooking time:
  nil
Serves 6

6 *small beetroots*
¾ *cup sour cream*
1 *tablespoon prepared horseradish*
1 *teaspoon coarse-grained mustard*
½ *cup cream*
¼ *cup mayonnaise*

½ *cup grated peeled apple*
¼ *teaspoon ground cloves*
fresh herbs for serving

1 Cook beetroot in boiling lightly salted water until just tender. Drain; peel and coarsely grate or cut into fine shreds. Pile onto a serving dish.
2 Combine sour cream, horseradish and mustard. Mix well.
3 Blend together cream, mayonnaise, apple and cloves in a separate bowl

and mix well.
4 To serve, spoon a generous amount of each sauce on the dish beside the beetroot (or serve sauces separately in bowls alongside). Garnish with herbs.

HINT
When buying beetroot look for beets with a good round shape, firm deep red skin and fresh clean tops.

49

Grilled Herbed Vegetables

Preparation time:
  40 minutes plus 1
  hour standing
Cooking time:
  8 minutes
Serves 8

2 *cloves garlic, crushed*
½ *cup olive oil*
2 *medium unpeeled*
  eggplants, cut into
  1 cm thick slices
4 *long zucchini, cut into*
  long strips 1 cm thick
1 *large red onion, cut in*
  1 cm thick slices
8 *large mushroom caps,*
  halved
4 *medium-sized ripe*
  tomatoes, halved
2 *each medium green*
  and red capsicum,
  seeded and quartered
2 *sprigs each fresh*
  marjoram, oregano,
  rosemary, sage, basil
  and thyme
freshly ground pepper

1 Add garlic to oil; let
stand 1 hour at room
temperature to mellow.
2 Sprinkle eggplant
slices with salt; let stand
on paper towels for 30
minutes. Rinse under
cold water; pat dry.
3 Brush eggplant and all
remaining vegetable
pieces with flavoured
oil.
4 Remove herb leaves
from sprigs (keep
separate). Chop leaves,
if large. Sprinkle
marjoram over eggplant;
oregano over zucchini;
rosemary over onion;
sage over mushrooms;
basil over tomatoes; and
thyme over capsicum.
Lightly sprinkle with
pepper.
5 Place all vegetables
directly on hot grill
about 15 cm above hot,
glowing coals (no
flames). Grill until crisp-
tender, turning as
needed 5–8 minutes.
Serve at once.

HINT
If you have a
rosemary bush, burn
a few branches on the
coals for added
flavour, or use a sprig
of rosemary as a
basting brush.

Grilled Herbed Vegetables

TEMPTING DESSERTS

Fruit Salad with Port

*D*esserts can be a fabulous finale to a barbecued meal. They can be as simple as a fresh seasonal fruit salad flavoured with liqueur or citrus juice or as self-indulgent as Lemon Meringue Pie.

We have given you some of our favourite sweet recipes, most of which can be made in advance. They feed large numbers easily and are not hard to make.

If you prefer to make use of your barbecue to serve a dessert, try the following ideas. Cook bananas in their skins on the hot plate or grill and, towards the end of cooking time when their skins begin to split, brush them with melted butter and brown sugar. Make mixed fruit kebabs, brushed with orange juice and butter, or wrap fresh sliced pears and berry fruits in foil, drizzle them with honey and serve them with toasted almonds and lashings of cream — the options are endless.

Fruit Salad with Port

Preparation time:
    20 minutes
Cooking time:
    nil
Serves 6

½ cup caster sugar
⅓ cup lemon juice
⅓ cup port
1 pawpaw, peeled and sliced
1 kiwi fruit, peeled and sliced
1 punnet raspberries
other seasonal fruit

1 Combine sugar, lemon juice and port in a screw-top jar. Shake well.
2 Combine all fruit in a serving bowl. Pour over dressing. Cover. Refrigerate until required. Serve with lashings of whipped cream.

Trifle

Preparation time:
    30 minutes plus setting time
Cooking time:
    nil
Serves 8

1 packet raspberry jelly
2 cups milk
4 tablespoons custard powder
2 teaspoons sugar
1 teaspoon vanilla essence
2 bananas
juice of ½ lemon

1 punnet strawberries, washed, hulled and sliced
1 x 425 g can unsweetened sliced peaches, drained
1 x 425 g can unsweetened apricot halves, drained
pulp of 2 passionfruit
200 mL cream, whipped

1 Prepare jelly following packet directions. Pour into a shallow dish. Allow to set in the refrigerator.
2 To prepare custard: in a saucepan, mix a little of the milk into the custard powder to form a smooth paste. Add sugar, pour in remaining milk and stir well.
3 Cook over a medium heat, stirring constantly, until custard boils and thickens. Reduce heat. Simmer for 3 minutes. Remove from heat. Stir in vanilla. Cool.
4 Peel and slice bananas. Sprinkle with lemon juice to prevent browning. Set aside.
5 To assemble Trifle: arrange half the fruit in layers in the base of a serving dish. Chop jelly roughly. Sprinkle half over the fruit. Cover with half of the custard. Continue layering until all ingredients are used, reserving some fruit for decoration.
6 Decorate with cream and fruit. Chill well before serving.

Pavlova

Preparation time:
  40 minutes
Cooking time:
  1¼ hours
Serves 8

4 *egg whites*
¾ *cup caster sugar*
1 *teaspoon lemon juice
  or vinegar*
pinch salt
300 *mL cream, whipped*
seasonal fruits

1 Beat egg whites until soft peaks form.

Gradually add sugar. Beat until stiff and glossy. Add lemon juice. Mix well.

2 Line an oven slide with baking paper or greased greaseproof paper. Spread mixture out roughly to make a 23 cm circle.

3 Bake in a slow oven (150°C) for 30 minutes. Reduce to very slow (120°C) for a further 45 minutes. Turn oven off. Allow Pavlova to cool in oven with door open.

4 Remove baking paper. Transfer to a serving platter. Top with whipped cream and a selection of fruits such as banana, strawberries, kiwi fruit and passionfruit.

HINT

Add sugar gradually and beat until all the sugar crystals have dissolved. Check that sugar has dissolved by rubbing a small amount of mixture between your fingers. If it is still gritty, continue beating.

Step 1

Step 2

Step 3

Step 4

Pavlova

Mango Ice-Cream

The ice-cream alone is wonderful, but it becomes a glamour dessert when garnished with chocolate leaves, frosted grapes and fresh mango slices.

Preparation time:
   30 minutes plus
   freezing time
Cooking time:
   nil
Serves 6

Ice-cream

2 cups cream
1 cup milk
1 cup puréed ripe mango
   (2 or 3 large)
1 cup sugar
1 tablespoon lemon or
   lime juice

Garnishes

few small clusters green
   grapes
1 egg white, lightly
   beaten
caster sugar
tiny ivy leaves
60–90 g dark chocolate
1 or 2 ripe mangoes,
   peeled and sliced

1 Combine cream, milk, puréed mango, sugar and lemon juice; mix together thoroughly.
2 If using a commercial ice-cream churn, pour mixture into canister and churn as manufacturer directs.

3 Otherwise, pour into freezer tray; freeze until mixture begins to set at the edges. Turn into a bowl; beat until light and fluffy. Return to tray; freeze until firm, but not rock-hard (see Hint).
4 Meanwhile, prepare garnishes; rinse and drain the grapes, break into small clusters and dry thoroughly on paper towels. Beat egg white lightly with fork. Brush white over grapes, then dip in sugar to coat. Let dry on wire rack.
5 For chocolate leaves choose tiny, well-shaped ivy leaves, wipe clean with damp paper and let dry. Melt chocolate and, using small brush or knife tip, spread over one side of each leaf. Let set, then carefully peel leaf off and discard. Store chocolate leaves in an airtight container.
6 To serve, scoop ice-cream on to dessert plates. Garnish with sugared grapes, chocolate leaves and thin mango slices.

> **HINT**
> For a lighter texture, fold one beaten egg white into mixture before final freezing.

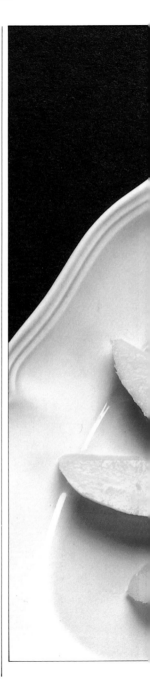

Mango Ice-Cream

Lemon Meringue Pie

Preparation time:
40 minutes plus
1 hour standing
Cooking time:
10 minutes
Serves 6

Pastry

1½ cups plain flour
1 tablespoon caster
sugar
125 g butter or
margarine, chopped
1 egg yolk
1 tablespoon cold water

Filling and Meringue

½ cup sugar
⅓ cup cornflour
1 cup water
grated rind of 2 lemons
½ cup lemon juice
3 eggs, separated
1 tablespoon butter
½ cup extra caster sugar

1 To make pastry:
combine flour and caster
sugar. Rub in butter
until crumbly. Beat
together egg yolk and
cold water, add to flour
mixture and mix to a
firm dough. Wrap and
chill until firm, about 1
hour. On lightly floured
surface, roll out dough
to line a 23 cm fruit pie
plate. Trim and decorate
rim as desired. Pierce
well with fork. Bake
blind at 220°C for 15
minutes, or until cooked

through and golden
brown. Cool.
2 To make filling:
combine ½ cup sugar
and the cornflour in
saucepan. Stir in water,
lemon rind and juice.
Cook and stir constantly
over moderately low
heat until thickened and
bubbly. Reduce heat and
simmer 2–3 minutes.
Remove from heat.
3 Beat egg yolks in small
bowl. Stir in a *little* of
the hot filling, then
return all to saucepan.
Cook, stirring, 2–3
minutes more. Stir in
butter, then pour into
pastry case.
4 To make meringue:
beat egg whites until
stiff. Gradually add
extra caster sugar,
beating constantly until
meringue forms stiff,

glossy peaks. Swirl
meringue over hot
filling, sealing
completely to pastry.
5 Bake at 220°C until
topping is golden, about
10 minutes. Cool
completely on wire rack.

HINT
To bake a flan 'blind',
line pierced pastry
with baking paper,
greaseproof paper or
foil. Fill with dry
beans, rice or ceramic
baking beads to
weigh down pastry.
Bake until firm, then
remove weights and
paper. Continue
baking until pastry is
evenly browned.

Step 1

Step 2

Step 3

Lemon Meringue Pie

Classic Fruit Flan

Classic Fruit Flan

Preparation time:
  1½ hours
Cooking time:
  15 minutes
Serves 8

Pastry

1 cup plain flour, sifted
1 tablespoon icing sugar
90 g butter or
  margarine, cut into
  pieces
1 egg yolk
1 tablespoon lemon juice

Filling

1¼ cups milk
1 egg
2 egg yolks
1 tablespoon plain flour
1 tablespoon cornflour
¼ cup caster sugar
1 teaspoon vanilla
  essence

Topping

1 punnet strawberries,
  washed and hulled

1 x 425 g can apricots,
  drained (reserve
  syrup)
2 kiwi fruit, peeled and
  sliced
1 tablespoon brandy
1 tablespoon arrowroot

1 To prepare pastry:
place flour in a large
bowl. Stir in icing sugar.
Add butter. Rub in,
using fingertips, until
mixture resembles
breadcrumbs.
2 Mix in egg yolk and
lemon juice. Press
together to form a soft
dough. Cover with
plastic wrap. Rest in the
refrigerator for 30
minutes.
3 Roll out between 2
sheets of plastic wrap or
on a lightly floured
surface until 3 mm thick.
Line a 23 cm flan dish
with pastry. Trim edges.
Refrigerate for 10
minutes. Prick base with
a fork. Bake in a hot

oven (200°C) for 10–15
minutes or until golden.
Cool.
4 To prepare filling:
whisk ¼ cup milk,
whole egg, yolks, flour,
cornflour and sugar
together in a small bowl.
In a saucepan, heat
remaining milk until
warm.
5 Whisk a little warm
milk into the egg
mixture. Pour the egg
mixture into the
remaining warm milk.
6 Return milk mixture
to heat. Heat, stirring
constantly, until mixture
boils and thickens.
Simmer for 3 minutes.
Blend in vanilla. Cool.
7 Spread custard over
base of pastry case.
Arrange fruit
decoratively on top.
8 Blend brandy into
reserved syrup. Stir a
little of the syrup
mixture into the
arrowroot to form a
smooth paste. Blend
paste into remaining
syrup. Heat, stirring
constantly, until mixture
boils and thickens.
Simmer for 3 minutes.
9 Brush warm glaze
over fruit. Refrigerate
until required.

HINT
When using a flan tin,
trim pastry from
edges by rolling your
rolling pin over the
rim.

Apples Poached in Wine

Preparation time:
  20 minutes plus 3
  hours standing
Cooking time:
  20 minutes
Serves 4

½ *cup currants*
1 ¼ *cups dry white wine*
¾ *cup water*
1 *cinnamon stick*
thinly slivered peel of
  1 *lemon or* 1 *small*
  orange
1 *tablespoon lemon juice*
4 *large green apples,*
  peeled, cored and
  sliced

1 Soak currants in bowl with enough boiling water to cover until plumped.

2 Meanwhile, in saucepan, heat wine, water, cinnamon, peel and lemon juice until boiling. Add half the apples, reduce heat and gently simmer until apples are semi-transparent, about 5 minutes.

3 Transfer apples with slotted spoon to glass bowl. Drain currants, rinse and add to wine mixture with remaining apples. Simmer about 5 minutes more. Pour mixture over apples in bowl.

4 Cool, cover and chill 2–3 hours. Remove cinnamon stick before serving.

Note. You can substitute plums, nectarines, peaches or pears for the apples if desired . . . or use a combination, as pictured.

HINT
Poached apples may also be served warm, topped with cream, for an autumn or winter barbecue.

Fruit Poached in Wine

61

THE BARBECUE FIRE

*P*eople *have been barbecuing ever since the discovery of fire, and the pastime, either as a way of entertaining or just plain relaxing, gets more and more popular. There are many types of barbecues on the market, but whether you choose a flat barbecue plate, a Hibachi or domed lidded grill, successful barbecues depend on slow burning embers, not scorching flames.*

Be sure to build the fire well in advance. The most popular fuel is charcoal, which burns slowly without spitting out sparks and gives an intense even heat. Wood can also be used — hardwoods are best. Let the fire burn down 30–45 minutes before you add the food. Coal and embers are ready when they turn ash-grey. At night they may have a red glow, but the ash-grey look is the best guide.

BARBECUE EQUIPMENT

There are a few pieces of barbecue equipment that every barbecue cook will need. Whatever utensils you choose make sure they are sturdy ones.

You will need:

● a long metal spatula with a durable handle for turning meats, burgers and delicate foods
● long-handled tongs to turn large cuts of meat
● a heavy-duty basting brush (a good quality paintbrush can be used for this)
● a jug to hold bastes, flavoured oils and marinades
● thick potholders or mitts
● a wire basket for holding, turning and cooking burgers or seafood
● a carving knife, fork and board
● heavy-duty foil for covering foods and keeping them warm.

SAFETY FIRST
Keep a first-aid kit nearby in case of burns.

CONTROLLING THE TEMPERATURE

Constant monitoring and control of temperature is very important for barbecuing. Gas and electric barbecues can be turned up or down or you can move food to cooler sides. You have just as much control with a charcoal fire because you can simply damp it down if it gets too hot. Damp the fire with water either from a very fine spray from your hose or by carefully sprinkling about a cup of water over the coals. This decreases the temperature immediately and puts moisture back into the food with rising steam. If your barbecue grill is rather close to the coals you may wish to move the food aside as you spray or sprinkle. Do not damp down a gas or electric barbecue.

Index